The Bonus Level

Artemis Drew

BookLeaf Publishing

India | USA | UK

Presentation by *BookLeaf Publishing*

Web: www.bookleafpub.com

E-mail: info@bookleafpub.com

ISBN: 9789358316582

First edition 2024

Dedicated to my dear Mother, Elizabeth, and my sister, PG, for supporting this side-quest; and to all those forging their own pathways.

ACKNOWLEDGEMENT

Before you all jump in, there is something I
must say
I want to thank some special ones for their help
along the way
This book, though short and sweet, it holds my
heart and all my care
And without their inspiration, my work would
not be written there:

My family, friends, and neighbors all contribute
to my light
They give me needed courage for all the things I
dare to write
But firstly, God himself, he gets me through
each living day
Without him I'd not be here to keep scribbling
away

I also thank my readers, you're the reason I hold
on
You'll have these words to cling to when one
day I will gone
My legacy in ink is scribed here for your benefit
So I hope you find what's needed as you peer
inside of it

And lastly, I thank trials and the pain that I've
gone through
They've shaped me as a person, and my
character, it grew
All these things in totality are the anchor to my
soul
So I continue with my journey marked down
here in versed scroll

The Bonus Level

I see you've found the bonus level
This booklet here for you
A twenty-one day odyssey
That I think was overdue

Surprise! It's not too long, I know
I hope you find all the same
Some words of comfort to see you through
And win life's momentous game

You've only just begun your quest
On your way to seek Ground Zero
But for now you must keep trekking on;
Must become your own hero

With diligence and grace you've fought
And for all your work thus far
I gift this page to readers loved;
Continue growing as you are!

You'll find that the tutorial
Is absent from your path—
A shame life lacks a manual
We'll just have to do the math

Yet fear not, such beloved ones
With each new step you take
That life is harder if never tried;
The ground rumbles in your wake

So carry on and do pack light
Take with you love and peace
The door to wonder opens now;
And at Zero we will meet

Chivalry Isn't Dead

Chivalry was never dead
The world, it just grew tired
They let their arms drop and they fled
From all that had transpired

We wish for knights in shining steel
And days of kings and queens
But for all the things we truly feel
We only live in dreams

"Idealists" as they like to say;
The "simple" few that care
They think we are naive that way
But they don't 'tempt to dare

To walk a narrow ethic line
And put all others first—
A lifestyle they wouldn't try;
To fail would hurt them worst

So I live on in spite of this
I do what most cannot
For I was born some centuries missed
But the code I ne'er forgot

The Universe is Breaking!

The universe is breaking!
It's bursting at the seems
The universe is breaking!
All into smithereens

The universe is breaking!
It's split 'twixt two extremes
The universe is breaking!
Yet no one sees, it seems

Our universe is breaking!
Can you and I not fix?
Our universe is breaking!
We fight with swords and sticks

Our universe is breaking!
Are we not to defend?
Our universe is breaking!
It looks like it's the end

Your universe is breaking!
Do you not even care?
Your universe is breaking
One day it won't be there

Your universe is breaking
This feels too much to bear
Your universe is breaking
Nothing in life is fair

My universe is breaking
I tried to tape the cracks
My universe is breaking
The pressure's on; it's stacked

My universe is breaking
Don't think I can go on
My universe is breaking
And with it I'll be gon—!

Lion Heart

All their lives they fight in battle
Listening to the constant prattle
Of the wicked ones who show their jaws
And torture the young with poisoned claws

Like lions they will steadfast stand
And bind together tight in bands
Their weapons of choice: hard work and zeal
To make their dreams so far away real

But they have waged war all their life
Doing what they can to make things right
Stronger in mind than they appear
A heart of gold begins to veer

Its righteous light to packs of pride
To draw back enemies who run to hide
A harder quest, but none will part;
They carry on with a Lion Heart

Writer's Block

Have you ever held a mystery
Inside your head and heart
That causes you such misery
When you aren't inspired by art

So many things to write and draw
So many things, so new
But my mind's decided to withdraw
From the things I used to do

A lack of motion inside my brain
I'm surprised I'm still awake
My muscles try but are dying to strain
And my hands are bound to break

So intricate a feeling, numb
A troublesome dose undue
To one who 'tempts to page become
But never made it through

Afraid

The future might be bright
That's what they always say
Then why am I afraid to fall
Afraid to breathe another day

I don't even want to be here
And I know that's hard to grasp
But not everyone is prepared for war
Not everyone will last

I have no clue what I'm doing
And I want to hold on to false hope
But my head and heart still speak the same
Telling me let go of the rope

It will only hurt for a second, I know
To free myself from life
But I lack all the will and the strength
To let my chest welcome the knife

I couldn't do it if I wanted to
There's something still tying me here
Holding me back like a conscience
Someone to keep my sight clear

I don't know where my weights lie
But they're stronger than I remember
Chaining me to earth so I
Can face my fears alone altogether

And I'm not afraid anymore
Because you can't compare your life to
another's
And if I've learned a single thing
Mine is way better than others

So don't forget what you have
Or where you had started from
But never lose sight of where you are going
Because the future can only come

Living in the past is futile
And turning the clock back: impossible
But never stop looking at where you are headed
Because what is brewing is unstoppable

Pressure

We're tumbled as we turn to change
Such diamonds in the rough
And though we toil endlessly
It's never good enough

Rare gems are formed by pressure, heat,
Good chemistry, and fate
But I'm tired of all the cuts and burns
No more of it I can take

For too much weight will break your bones
And crush your aching heart
It's spinning now, I pray it stops
Or I'm bound to fall apart

Sinking

Should depression be a sinking ship
My head is underwater
The waves come in without consent;
I gave no imprimatur

"High-functioning" is hidden death
Can't see it, but it's there
Not mentioned in the medic books
There's no coming up for air

I bottle it, can't take much more
It spills out when I break
And keeps on going until I'm gone
See, my suffering isn't fake

Wavering, I'll tread the deep;
I really have little choice
I speak for ones wanting to quit
And those left without a voice

We all feel like we're going down
Whilst not captains of our boats
But we save face and hide our frowns
To try and stay afloat

People

I think of all the people
Who are living worse than I:
There's Army, Air Force, Navy
Breathing by a battle cry

There's homeless, sick, and destitute
The desperate and the lame
Who've accepted all there is
Or have tried to play the game

We've strugglers, hopeless, wrathful
They're all trying to get ahead
But the world has put them down
Too long; they'd rather be in bed

The abandoned, masked, addicted
Those are trapped with slim escape
They bet all their wins on chances
Just to grasp a better place

We've got tells, some ticks; we're injured
We bear all the little things:
Hardships, horrors, and mishaps
Just the thought makes our eyes sting

So you see, we've all a story
And the trick is how we tell
There's no quest for gold or glory;
For the grave is where we dwell

Writing the Wrongs

There's so many stressors to be found in this
world
And as we grow older the worst gets unfurled
So what does one do when you've nowhere to
go
and side-quests unconquered have left you to
woe?

To right all the wrongs and escape these
deadlands
The best ways I've found are through prayer and
by hand;
My tears reach the heavens and God then takes
note
And I'm comforted then through the scriptures
He wrote

So I follow those footsteps and take up my pen
To write my way out and find spirit again
The books always listen, they don't turn you
away
And should you share secrets, unspoken they'll
stay

The ink marks my sorrows that pierce through
the soul
And once the words dry, I feel hollowed, yet
whole
For sometimes the sadness that dwells in the
heart
Needs to be vented so that I can restart

Spontaneous

Have you ever eaten circus nuts
Or played a plastic flute?
Did you buy new soda at the store
Or spend a day being mute?

Have you tried to ice skate with a friend
Instead of rollerblades?
Or crafted candles from your home
And put them on display?

Have you ever put a record on
And let the music play?
Or listened to the radio
Without touching your phone all day?

Have you climbed a mountain big and tall
Or traveled out of state?
If you haven't, I'd give it a whirl
Before it's all too late

Do try dessert as breakfast first
Or a scavenger hunt in-store
You'll find with each new thing you try
You haven't had this much fun before

If you've never done one of these things
Then go, this is your chance!
Try being a little spontaneous
And you may truly live, perchance

Shattered

Shattered like a piece of glass
But the crash, it set me free;
Hit the bottom but now I laugh
There's more perspectives to see

I gathered them all one by one
You don't know this newer me;
I'm stronger than I ever was before
I put back the pieces differently

The Consoling

I see the mountains you have climbed
And all the ones ahead
I see them in the way you smile
To hide the truth instead

Your gait is weary, no sleep at all
The nights lack peace and rest
But still you rise up to the call
And give us each your best

The truth is that you're suffering
From a world that's left you cold
And when the winds go blustering
You splinter and unfold

A path untracked, a journey long
There's so much left to do
And yet the heart, it's lonely song
Is pouring out of you

But that's the thing they'll never see
As we come and take our seats
You brace yourself and let it be—
Won't let us see defeat

My mental powers fight entropy;
To console is what I seek
But don't be scared of this entity
Your secrets I will keep

I'll try to heal your soul within
And compassion warmly share
This reckoning will do you in
So lean on those who care

Tethered

I glance back at days that do not exist
I'm beyond them; they've fallen from time
Yet sometimes I travel back into the past
And find tangents of an angrier line

Some feelings I had as a child are missing
They've evolved, so I think, and matured
And I rarely recall those emotions to mind
(My receding memory is assured)

There are no pictures to support the frame
That I grew out of long ago
But the problems remain, the answers aren't
clear
And where I'll go next I don't know

I've somehow been tethered to old memories
They keep to the back of my mind
Tying me down to perceptions outdated
Thus I navigate "New" undefined

This gruesome experience I carry along
It's too much to lug around everywhere
But without it I fear that I'd never learn
So I'm stuck with those burdens to bear

The Return of Everything

I feel hopeless in the winter
When life all is dead and gone
The trees are stripped of color
With early pullback from the dawn

The woods are drenched in darkness
As clouds cover up the sky
No blue graces the horizon
And the land is frozen dry

It only snows this season
When not enough to get stuck in
And fronts blow in without warning
 In their haste, my skin grows thin

I'm never ready for the cold air
It's just enough to make me snap
The tundra sinks into my bare bones
I'd rather bundle up and nap

And the sun sets way too early
I don't get sunsets anymore
Where I'd enough time to enjoy them
I've got too much to run for

The whole landscape is a wasteland
So I wait patiently for Spring
Until then, I'll stay indoors
And await the return of everything

For All of Us

The world is strung up by a single thread
And it's starting to unravel
But no one person holds the loom
So the chaos starts to spread

We race forward to the end of time
To try and fix the past
Weaving through each crisis fast
Before the last hour chimes

There's no instructions for these things
Life is messy and uncontrolled
In the meantime we just hold our breaths
To see what the future will bring

A sacrifice, it must be made
Which one of us will bear the cost?
The price for stability, a steeper loss
So existence itself doesn't fade

I'll take this stake, yes, me alone
I'll do this for all of us
No one will miss me when I'm gone
You're shocked, but you should've known

I think I was always meant for this
The last missing piece of this puzzle
Missing but not lost, simply out of the game
To save infinity from the endless abyss

And that, dear friends, is the most I can do
You'll have to shoulder the rest on your own
But don't look back— you don't need to;
Keep going and see my surrender through

The Imagineer

There's an old shop in town where nobody goes
We don't know how the business stays afloat
But it's shaped like a bird- no -or maybe a boat?
The point is is that nobody knows

The forge lies away at the end of the road
Sounds lonely, but she likes it that way
The inventor, I mean; never envied the fray
She prefers to stick by her own abode

If you go anyway, you might find the woman
She runs the whole place alone— always has
Take a peek inside at her trinkets, pizzazz;
The miracles in there are inhuman!

If you need something made, something fixed or
reformed
Just stop by and let the girl know
The Imagineer is a genius inventor; watch her
go!
No commission has she scorned

She can make anything that she dreams come to
life
It's a gift very rare in this world

And the shop changes faces, it whooshes and
whirls
As she works until she gets it right

People think it's amazing or they think that it's
weird
It's just simply too good to be true
But I've found that complexity isn't anything
new
And the real ones are as they appear

So stop by if you're free, perhaps give it a
chance
You may gain something priceless in turn
To imagine is key in a world full of rules
We should always be ready to learn

Counterclockwise

It started with a waste of time
I saw a clock, grandfather tall
To leave from here would be a crime
But I didn't feel bad at all

I grabbed a stool and climbed on top
I saw the dial through the glass
Then held the hands until time stopped;
No seconds more would pass

I turned them back and then they broke
My life reversed, and I was cursed
The spinning ceased— I almost choked
For a moment I thought the worst

To relive all that I had seen;
Mistakes were made, could be redone
Good moments played like theatre scenes
Refined or purely re-run

A cycle of pretending starts
Replay the game from Level One
To imitate those beating hearts
A feat that can't be done

It went like this for quite a while
From day to day, can't count the lies
I tell you fools, avoid this trial:
Don't live counterclockwise

Fated

The quick are not always a step ahead
The ones taught to battle are down or they're
dead
The brave wielding swords don't always win the
fight
Nor do the wise ones always find the light

The ambitious do not always gain the wealth
Nor are the doctors always good in health
And never does a man escape when death nears
Because time kills us all with his hands as his
spears

Just as the fish are snared in a net
The birds once singing were taken by a threat
For a man knows not his day nor does he the
hour
And never got to be the one holding all the
power

Last

Unwavering fear that all will hold
Whether or not the truth be told
That all will run but hide in vain
From pain that will soon come again

Fight to the death or rise to the test
Or to what haunts you thou shalt be left
Loneliness one or Crowds another
Sister Space or Clustered brother

Night and Lost are sibling terrors
Let not imagination be your error
For the unknown is only what you will see
Soon to come and whisper unease

So carry on and keep your head
Or to your nightmares you will be fed
The advice I hold to those dead last:
Be strong, be brave, and to these steadfast

Speak, Infinity!

To speak is to connect the earth
And have all meaning shared
Be one with ground and sea and sky;
Harmoniously paired

This never-ending heart-to-heart
We equally cultivate
Through history and present part
To expand our mental states

But words are more than active talk
With power they are imbued
When used well, we can change the world
For our better and find the truth

We all are one; one speaks for all
You add a little more
So go and speak, Infinity!
It's a wide and open door

www.ingramcontent.com/pod-product-compliance
Lightning Source LLC
LaVergne TN
LVHW010942200726
843509LV00013B/2273